WORD by WORD

Songbook

What's Your Name?	Fashion
Great Big World	Working
Another Day	Going to the Beach
In My House	Power Up
The City	Word by Word
Supermarket Sally	

A B C D E F G H I J K
1 2 3 4 5 6 7 8 9 10 11

VOLUME I

Peter Bliss
Steven J. Molinsky • Bill Bliss

Prentice Hall Regents

Publisher: *Tina Carver*
Director of Production and Manufacturing: *David Riccardi*
Editorial Production/Design Manager: *Dominick Mosco*
Interior Design, Production Supervision, and Page Composition: *Ken Liao*
Electronic Art: *Todd Ware* and *Rolando Corujo*
Production Coordinator: *Ray Keating*
Cover Coordinator: Merle Krumper

Illustrations: *Richard E. Hill*

Printed in the United States of America

10   9   8   7   6   5   4   3

ISBN 0-13-064767-5

CONTENTS

The *Word by Word Songbook* and accompanying *Song Album* offer entertaining practice with English vocabulary through a variety of popular musical styles. They may be used independently or as musical accompaniments to the *Word by Word* family of Picture Dictionaries: *Word by Word, Word by Word Basic*, and the *Word by Word Bilingual Editions*.

Volume I of the *Songbook* and *Song Album* features 11 original songs that highlight useful English vocabulary:

What's Your Name?	Personal Information and Family Members
Great Big World	Countries, Nationalities, and Languages
Another Day	Everyday Activities
In My House	Rooms in the Home
The City	Places Around Town
Supermarket Sally	Food Shopping
Fashion	Clothing
Working	Occupations and Work Activities
Going to the Beach	Recreation
Power Up	Sport and Exercise Actions
Word by Word	"The Language Learner's Theme"

Each song appears twice on the album – first, with the words and music; and then in a "karaoke-style" sing-along version with just the musical background.

The Songbook highlights include:

♪ Full-page color illustrations that tell the story of each song through pictures. *(Look at the illustrations as you listen and sing along!)*

♪ The lyrics for each song. *(Read the lyrics as you listen and sing along!)*

♪ A "fill-in" version of the lyrics. *(Listen to the song and write in the missing words!)*

♪ Exercises and activities. *(Practice vocabulary as you answer questions, create new songs, and have fun learning English through music!)*

♪ The complete sheet music for each song. *(Sing along with a guitar or piano on your own or with friends!)*

The *Word by Word Song Album* is available in cassette and CD versions. So pop in your cassette or CD, open your songbook, and get ready to make some music as you learn English with the *Word by Word Song Album*!

Dedicated to language learners and their teachers,
who bring the world a little closer together . . .
word by word.

2

WHAT'S YOUR NAME?

(Chorus)
What's your name?
Where do you live?
What's your address?
I'd like to say, "Hello. How do you do?"
Oh-oh-oh-oh!
I'd like to introduce myself to you.

If I want to talk to you on the telephone,
What number should I call?
I could ask the operator for "Information, please!"
But I don't know your name at all!

Chorus (2x)

Let's take a walk on over to my house
And meet my family.
I live in this apartment with
My father and mother,
My sister and brother,
My niece and nephew . . .
There are more, let me tell you!
My uncle and aunt.
I know you think we can't all fit,
But we're a close family, you see.

What's your name? (What's your name?)
Where do you live? (Where do you live?)
What's your address?
I'd like to say, "Hello. How do you do?"
Oh-oh-oh-oh!
I'd like to introduce myself to you.
I'd like to say, "Hello. How do you do?"

I'd like to introduce myself to you.

WHAT'S YOUR NAME?

What's your _____?
Where do you _____?
What's your _____?
I'd like to say, "_____. How do you do?"
Oh-oh-oh-oh!
I'd like to _____ myself to you.

> If I want to talk to you on the _____,
> What _____ should I call?
> I could ask the _____ for "Information, please!"
> But I don't know your _____ at all!

What's _____ name?
Where do _____ live?
What's _____ address?
I'd like to say, "Hello. How do _____ do?"
Oh-oh-oh-oh!
I'd like to introduce myself to _____.

> Let's take a walk on over to my _____
> And meet my _____.
> I live in this _____ with
> My _____ and _____,
> My _____ and _____,
> My _____ and _____ . . .
> There are more, let me tell you!
> My _____ and _____.
> I know you think we can't all fit,
> But we're a close _____, you see.

_____ your name?
_____ do you live?
_____ your address?
I'd like to say, "Hello. _____ do you do?"
Oh-oh-oh-oh!
I'd like to introduce myself to you.
I'd like to say, "Hello. _____ do you do?"

I'd like to introduce myself to you.

In this song there are three ways to greet somebody. Can you find them?

1. _____ .

2. _____ _____ _____ _____?

3. _____ _____ ____ _____ _____ _____ _____ .

Who does the singer live with? Unscramble the family members.

1. rfheta   _____

2. tuan   _____

3. icene   _____

4. cleun   _____

5. ohmtre   _____

6. reists   _____

7. penwhe   _____

8. rtrhbeo   _____

What's your name? . . . .

Where do you live? . . . .

What's your address? . . . .

If I want to talk to you on the telephone, what number should I call? . . . .

If you want to find out somebody's telephone number, what can you do? . . . .

. . . .

Who lives with you? . . . .

Tell about all the people in your family: Who are they? Where do they live? . . . .

. . . .

. . . .

. . . .

. . . .

What do you think a *close family* means? . . . .

. . . .

Do you have a *close family?* . . . .

. . . .

What's Your Name?

Words and Music by
PETER S. BLISS

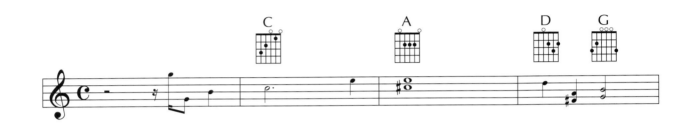

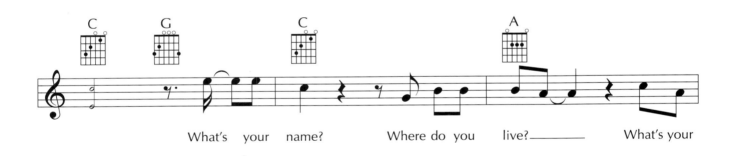

What's   your   name?   Where do you   live?_____   What's your

ad - dress?   I'd   like to say,   "Hel-lo.   How do you   do?"_____   Oh- oh-

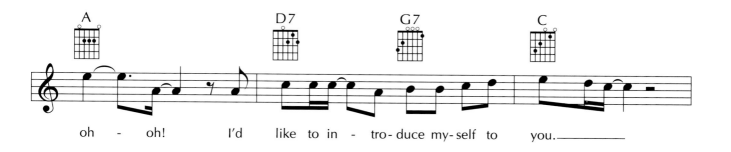

oh - oh! I'd like to in - tro - duce my - self to you._____

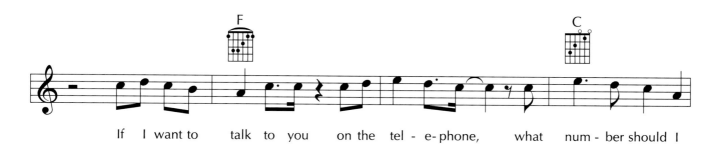

If I want to talk to you on the tel - e - phone, what num - ber should I

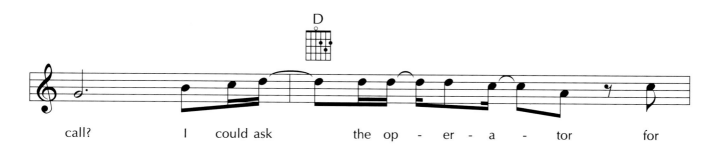

call? I could ask the op - er - a - tor for

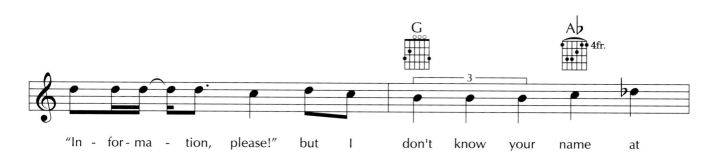

"In - for - ma - tion, please!" but I don't know your name at

all! What's your name? Where do you live?_____ What's your

ad - dress? I'd like to say, "Hel-lo. How do you do?"_____ Oh- oh -

oh - oh! I'd like to in - tro- duce my-self to you._____ What's your

name? *(What's your name?)* Where do you live? *(Where do you live?)*_____ What's your

ad - dress? I'd like to say, "Hel-lo. How do you do?"_____ Oh- oh-

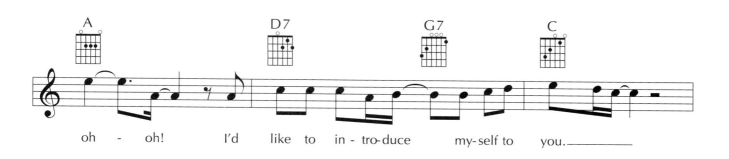

oh - oh! I'd like to in-tro-duce my-self to you._____

Let's take a walk on ov-er to my__ house and meet my fam-i -

ly. I live in this a - part-ment with my fath-er and moth-er, my

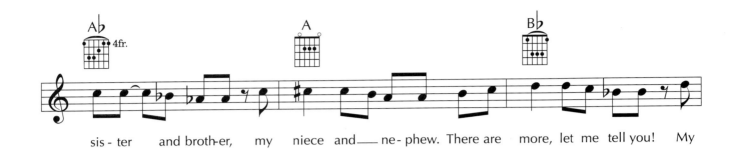

sis - ter and broth-er, my niece and— ne - phew. There are more, let me tell you! My

un - cle and aunt. I know you think we can't all fit, but we're a close fam - i -

ly, you see. What's your name? *(What's your name?)* Where do you

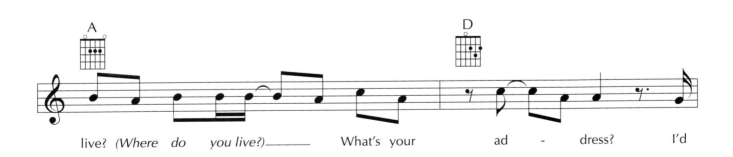

live? *(Where do you live?)*——— What's your ad - dress? I'd

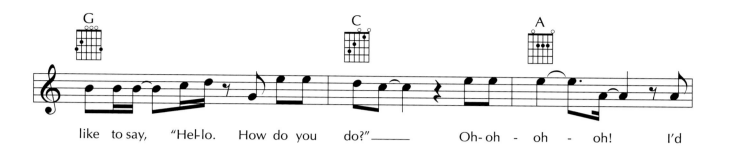

like to say, "Hel-lo. How do you do?"_____ Oh-oh - oh - oh! I'd

like to in - tro-duce my - self to you._____ I'd

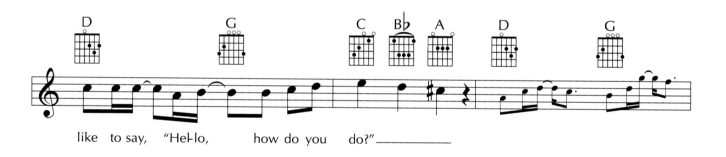

like to say, "Hel-lo, how do you do?"_____

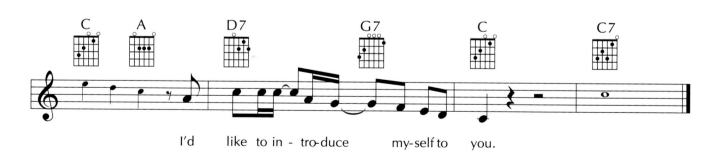

I'd like to in - tro-duce my-self to you.

GREAT BIG WORLD

(Chorus)
It's a great big world, a great big world!
Oceans, continents . . . a great big world!
It's a great big world, a great big world!
So many places in this great big world!

> You can drive from North America
> All the way to South America,
> Take a boat east to Africa,
> Then go south to Antarctica.

> You can sail the Atlantic,
> You can take a trip to Europe,
> Go to the Middle East and Asia,
> Sail the Pacific to Australia.

Chorus (2x)

> Tell me, "What's your native language?
> And what country are you from?"
> We live together in this great big world.
> It's a home to everyone!

Chorus (2x)

GREAT BIG WORLD

It's a great big _____, a great big _____!
Oceans, _____ . . . a great big world!
It's a great _____ world, a _____ big world!
So many _____ in this great big world!

    You can _____ from North America
    All the way to _____ _____,
    Take a _____ east to Africa,
    Then go _____ to Antarctica.

    You can sail the _____,
    You can take a trip to _____,
    Go to the Middle East and _____,
    Sail the _____ to Australia.

It's _____ great big world, _____ great big world!
_____, continents . . . a great big world!
It's a great big _____, a great big world!
So many places _____ this great big world!

    Tell me, "What's your native _____?
    And what _____ are you from?"
    We live _____ in this great big world.
    It's a _____ to everyone!

_____ a great big world, a great big world!
Oceans, continents . . . _____ great big world!
_____ a great big world, a great big world!
So _____ places in this great big world!

IS IT TRUE?

Circle True or False.

1.	You can drive from North America to Africa.	True	False
2.	You can drive from South America to North America.	True	False
3.	You can take a boat north to Antarctica.	True	False
4.	You can sail the Atlantic from North America to Europe.	True	False
5.	You can sail the Atlantic to Australia.	True	False

ABOUT YOU

What country are you from? . . . .

What continent is your country part of? . . . .

What countries can you drive to from your country? . . . .

Can you sail anywhere from your country? Where? . . . .

What ocean or sea is near your country? . . . .

What countries have you visited? How did you get there? What did you do there? . . . .

. . . .

. . . .

What country do you want to visit in the future? How will you get there? What will you do there? . . . .

. . . .

. . . .

Some people say that in pictures from space, our *great big world* looks more like a *big blue marble*. What do you think this means? . . . .

. . . .

. . . .

SILLY SONG

Fill in the verses using any continents, countries, and bodies of water. (You can use pages 6-7 of the *Word by Word Picture Dictionary* for ideas.) Then sing your song using the sing-along version of "Great Big World" on the *Word by Word Song Album*.

You can drive from . . . .

All the way to . . . .,

Take a boat east to . . . .,

Then go south to . . . .

You can sail the . . . .,

You can take a trip to . . . .,

Go to . . . . and . . . .,

Sail the . . . . to . . . .

Great Big World

Words and Music by
PETER S. BLISS

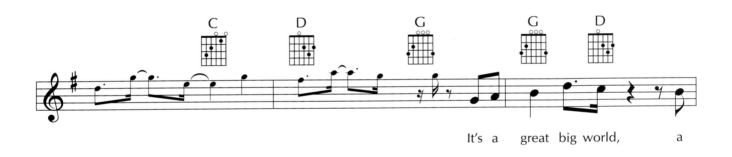

It's a   great big world,   a

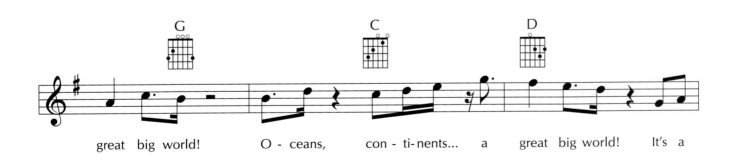

great big world!   O - ceans,   con - ti - nents... a   great big world!   It's a

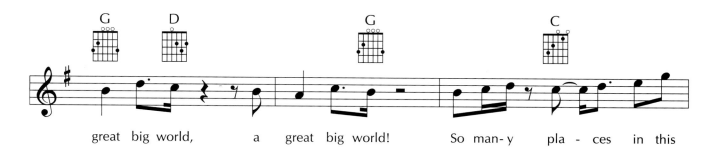

great big world, a great big world! So man-y pla - ces in this

great big world! You can drive from North A - mer - i - ca

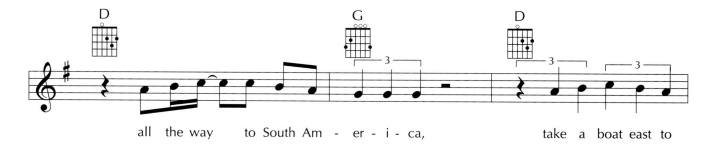

all the way to South Am - er - i - ca, take a boat east to

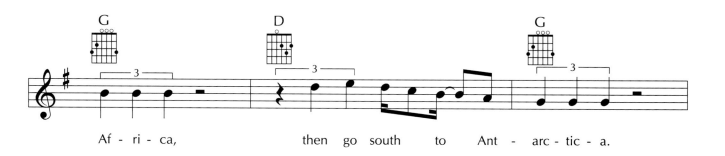

Af - ri - ca, then go south to Ant - arc - tic - a.

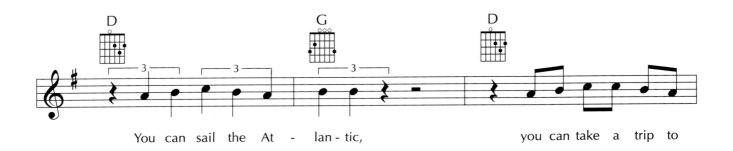

You can sail the At - lan - tic, you can take a trip to

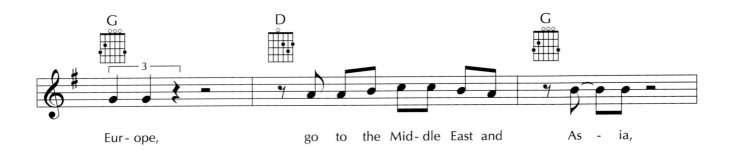

Eur - ope, go to the Mid - dle East and As - ia,

sail the Pa - ci - fic to Aus - tral - ia. It's a great big world, a

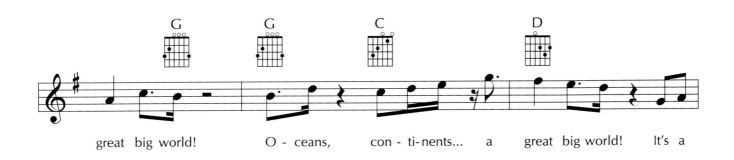

great big world! O - ceans, con - ti - nents... a great big world! It's a

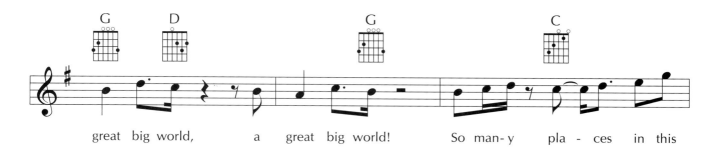

great big world, a great big world! So man-y pla - ces in this

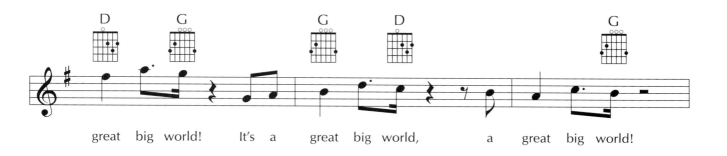

great big world! It's a great big world, a great big world!

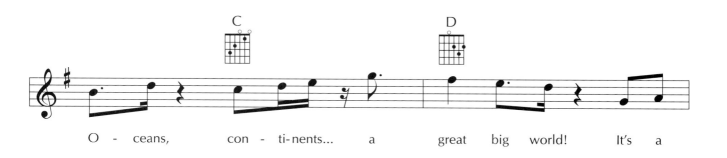

O - ceans, con - ti-nents... a great big world! It's a

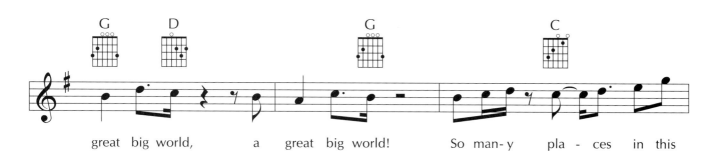

great big world, a great big world! So man-y pla - ces in this

great big world!   Tell me, "What's your nat - ive   lan - guage?

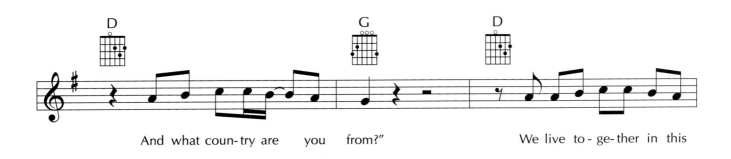

And what coun-try are   you   from?"   We live to - ge-ther in this

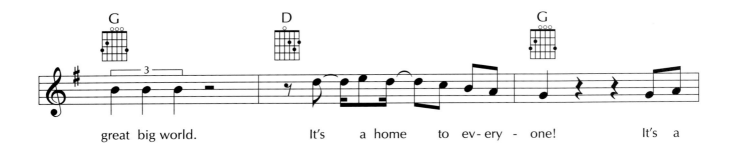

great big world.   It's   a   home   to ev- ery - one!   It's a

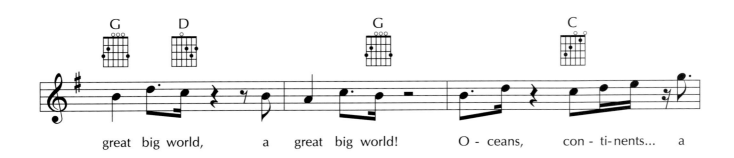

great big world,   a   great big world!   O - ceans,   con - ti-nents... a

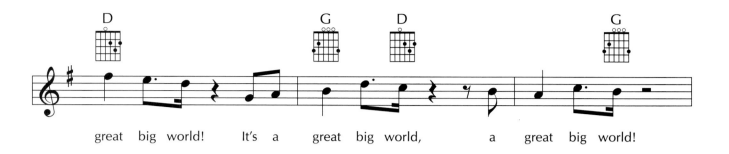

great big world! It's a great big world, a great big world!

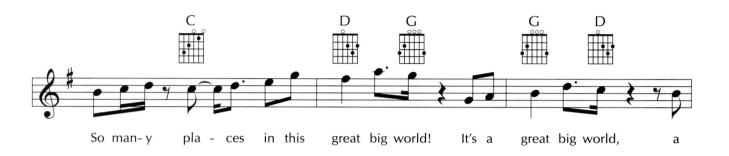

So man-y pla - ces in this great big world! It's a great big world, a

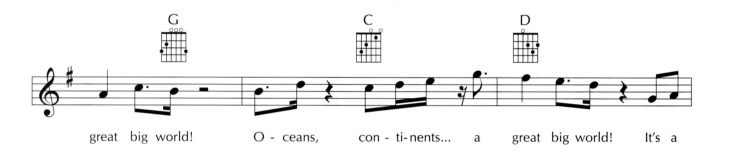

great big world! O - ceans, con - ti - nents... a great big world! It's a

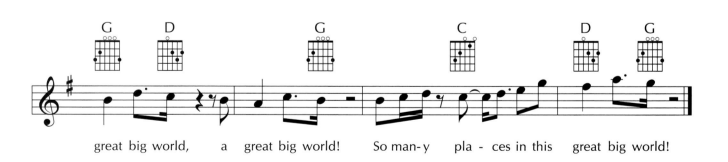

great big world, a great big world! So man-y pla - ces in this great big world!

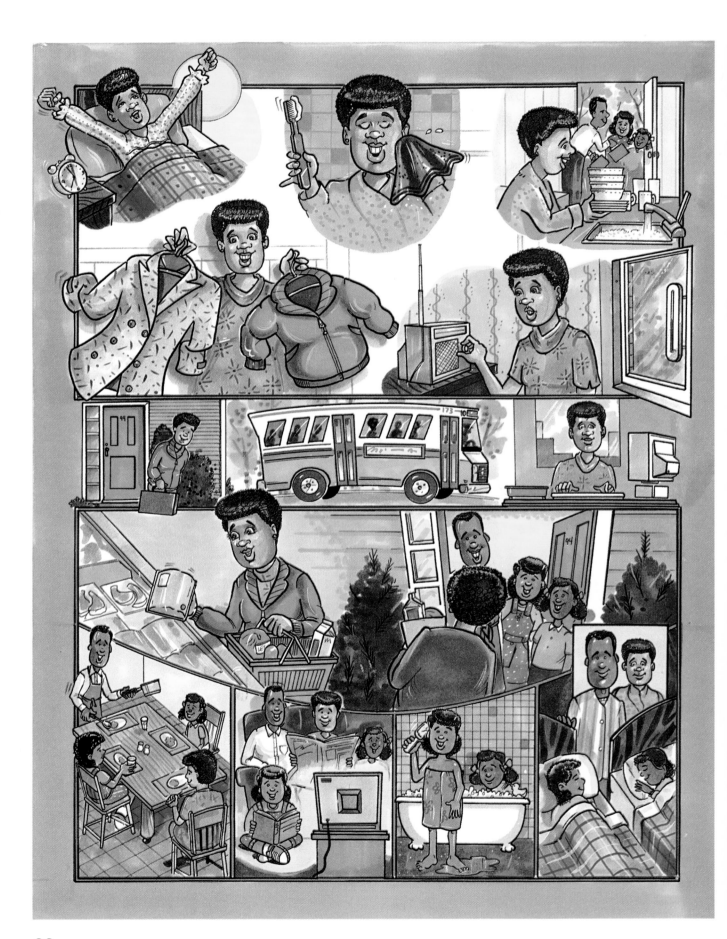

ANOTHER DAY

It's another day . . . woh – woh . . . another day!
It's time to work! No time for play!
It's another day!

"Good morning! It's time to get up!"
The sun shines in my eyes.
It's time to brush my teeth, wash my face,
Stack the breakfast dishes high!

What clothes should I be wearing?
That's when I turn on the radio.
I listen to what the weatherman says,
And it's off to work I go!

It's another day . . . woh – woh . . . another day!
It's time to work! No time for play!
It's another day!

Another day . . . woh – woh . . . another day!
When one day ends, one begins again.
It's another day!

After work I pick up dinner
At the local grocery store.
Then I go home to my family.
They greet me at the door.

We all sit down for dinner.
Then we read or watch TV.
We take our baths and say goodnight,
All sleeping peacefully.

It's another day . . . woh – woh . . . another day!
It's time to work! No time for play!
It's another day!

Another day . . . woh – woh . . . another day!
When one day ends, one begins again.
It's another day!
Another day!

ANOTHER DAY

It's another _____ . . . woh – woh . . . another _____!
It's time to _____! No time for _____!
It's another day!

    "Good _____! It's time to _____ _____!"
    The _____ shines in my eyes.
    It's time to _____ my teeth, _____ my face,
    Stack the _____ dishes high!

    What _____ should I be wearing?
    What's when I turn on the _____.
    I _____ to what the weatherman says,
    And it's off to _____ I go!

It's another day . . . woh – woh . . . _____ day!
It's _____ to work! No _____ for play!
It's another day!

Another day . . . woh - woh . . . another day!
When one day _____, one _____ again.
It's another day!

    After work I pick up _____
    At the local grocery _____.
    Then I go _____ to my family.
    They greet me at the _____.

    We all sit down for _____.
    Then we _____ or watch TV.
    We take our _____ and say goodnight,
    All _____ peacefully.

It's another day . . . woh – woh . . . another day!
_____ time to work! _____ time for play!
It's another day!

Another day . . . woh – woh . . . another day!
When one day ends, one begins _____.
It's another day!
Another day!

IS IT TRUE?

Circle True or False.

1. It's a cloudy day.   True   False
2. The singer had breakfast today.   True   False
3. The singer lives alone.   True   False
4. This family sometimes watches TV after dinner.   True   False
5. The singer listens to the radio in the morning.   True   False

RHYME TIME

What's the rhyming word from the song?

1. play   _____
2. go   _____
3. peacefully   _____
4. door   _____

WE BELONG TOGETHER

Match the words.

____ 1. stack   a. bath
____ 2. wear   b. radio
____ 3. listen   c. goodnight
____ 4. watch   d. clothes
____ 5. take   e. TV
____ 6. say   f. dishes

ABOUT YOU

What time do you get up? ....

What do you do before you leave home in the morning? ....

....

How do you decide what to wear? ....

....

How do you find out the weather forecast? ....

When you go home, does anybody greet you at the door? Who? ....

What time do you usually have dinner? ....

What do you usually have for dinner? ....

Who do you have dinner with? ....

Do you like to watch TV? What programs do you watch? ....

....

What do you usually do after dinner? ....

What time do you go to sleep? ....

Another Day

Words and Music by
PETER S. BLISS

It's an-o-ther day...

woh - woh... an-o-ther day! It's

time to work! No time for play! It's an-o-ther day!

"Good morn-ing! It's time to get up!" The

sun shines in my eyes. It's time to brush my teeth,

wash my face, stack the break-fast dish - es high! What

clothes should I be wear - ing? That's when I turn on the rad - i - o.

an - o - ther day! When one day ends, one be -

gins a - gain. It's an - o - ther day!

Af- ter

work I pick up din - ner at the lo - cal gro - cery store.

Then I go home to my fam - i - ly. They

greet me at the door.   We all sit down for din-

ner.   Then we   read   or watch   T   V.   We

take   our baths   and   say good-night,   all   sleep-ing   peace-ful-ly.—

_____   It's an - o - ther   day...

woh - woh...   an - o - ther   day!   It's

time to work! No time for play! It's an-o-ther day! An-o-ther day... woh - woh... an-o-ther day! When one day ends, one be - gins a-gain. It's an-o-ther day! An-o-ther day!

IN MY HOUSE

In my house, in my house
There's a living room with a fireplace.
There's a cozy couch next to a tall bookcase
In my house, in my house.

In my house, in my house
There's a dining room where everybody eats.
There's a table with a flower centerpiece
In my house, in my house.

It's so nice to come home,
Wherever home may be.
A place that feels safe and warm
For you and me, and a family.

In my house, in my house
There's a kitchen with an oven and a sink,
A refrigerator full of things to eat and drink
In my house, in my house.

In my house, in my house
There's a baby's room we call the nursery.
There's a bathroom with a mirror above the vanity
In my house, in my house.

It's so nice to come home,
Wherever home may be.
A place that feels safe and warm
For you and me, and a family.

In my house, in my house
There's a bedroom with a giant king-size bed
With two fluffy pillows and a quilted spread
In my house, in my house.

Oh! In my house, in my house!
Oh! In my house, in my house!

IN MY HOUSE

In my _____, in my house
There's a _____ _____ with a fireplace.
There's a cozy _____ next to a tall bookcase
In my house, in my house.

In _____ house, in _____ house
There's a _____ _____ where everybody eats.
There's a _____ with a flower centerpiece
In my house, in my house.

    It's so nice to come _____,
    Wherever home may be.
    A place that feels safe and warm
    For _____ and _____, and a family.

In my house, in my house
There's a _____ with an oven and a _____,
A _____ full of things to eat and drink
In my house, in my house.

In my house, in my house
There's a baby's room we call the _____.
There's a _____ with a mirror above the vanity
In my house, in my house.

    It's so _____ to come home,
    Wherever _____ may be.
    A place that feels safe and warm
    For you and me, and a _____.

In my house, in my house
There's a _____ with a giant king-size bed
With two fluffy _____ and a quilted spread
In my house, in my house.

Oh! In my house, in my house!
Oh! In my house, in my house!

WHERE CAN I FIND YOU?

In which room can you find these things?

1. king-size bed _____
2. refrigerator _____
3. vanity _____
4. fireplace _____
5. table _____
6. oven _____
7. pillow _____
8. couch _____

IT MAKES NO SENSE TO ME

Check the word combinations that don't make sense.

____ 1. fluffy oven   ____ 4. cozy centerpiece
____ 2. tall bookcase   ____ 5. full refrigerator
____ 3. safe place   ____ 6. quilted kitchen

ABOUT YOU

What kind of home do you live in? . . . .

How many rooms are there? . . . .

Is there a living room? Tell about it. . . . .

. . . .

Where do you usually eat? . . . .

What's in your kitchen? . . . .

. . . .

How many bathrooms are there? . . . .

How many bedrooms are there? . . . .

DRAW ME A PICTURE

Draw a picture of the place where you live. Show the rooms and items of furniture.

In My House

Words and Music by
PETER S. BLISS

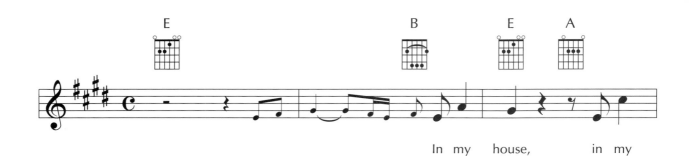

In my house, in my

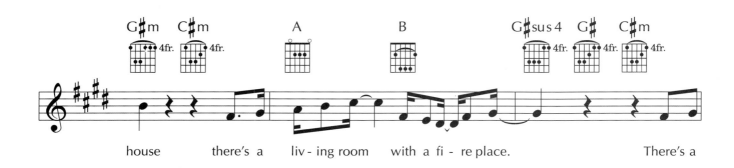

house there's a liv-ing room with a fi-re place. There's a

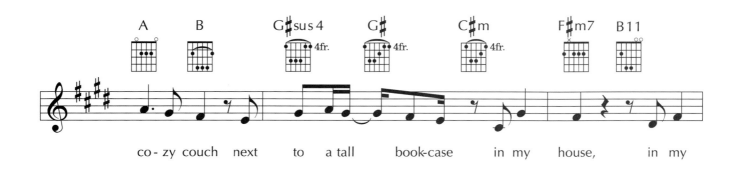

co-zy couch next to a tall book-case in my house, in my

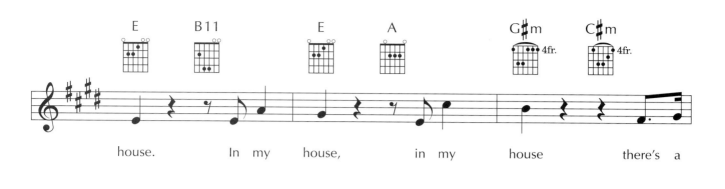

house. In my house, in my house there's a

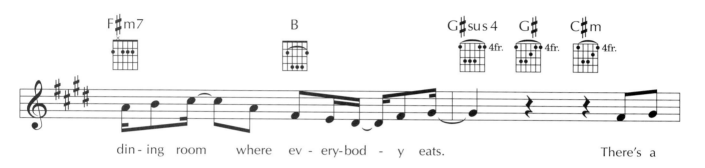

din - ing room where ev - ery-bod - y eats. There's a

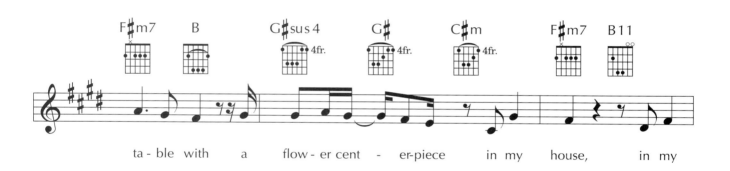

ta - ble with a flow - er cent - er-piece in my house, in my

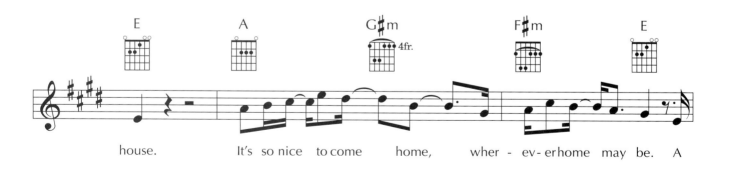

house. It's so nice to come home, wher - ev - er home may be. A

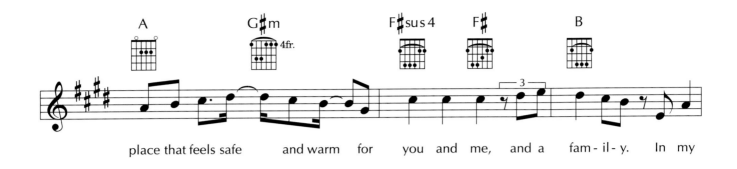

place that feels safe and warm for you and me, and a fam-il-y. In my

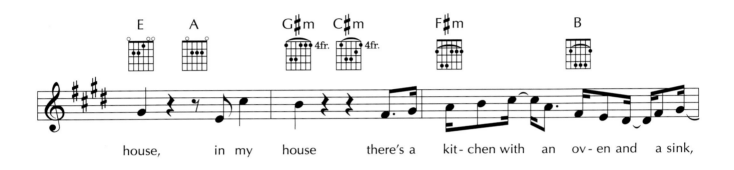

house, in my house there's a kit-chen with an ov-en and a sink,

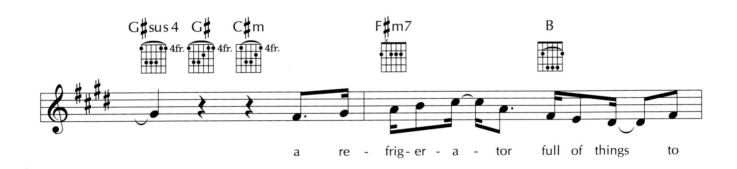

a re-frig-er-a-tor full of things to

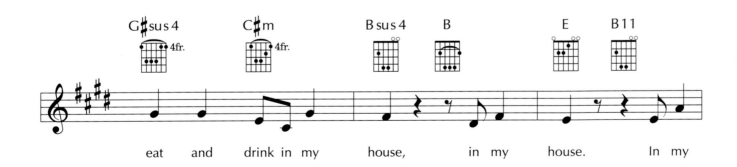

eat and drink in my house, in my house. In my

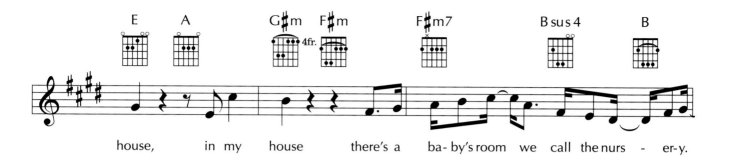

house,   in my house   there's a   ba- by's room   we call the nurs - er-y.

There's a bath - room with   a mir - ror a -

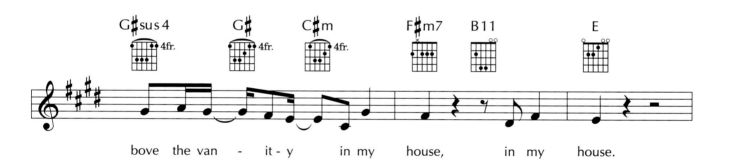

bove the van - it-y   in my house,   in my   house.

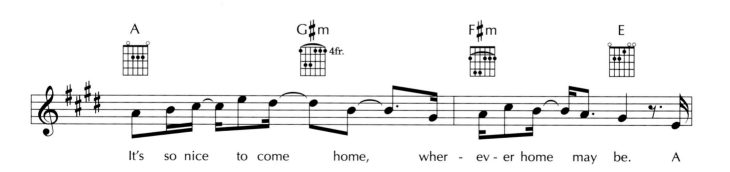

It's so nice   to come   home,   wher - ev - er home may be.   A

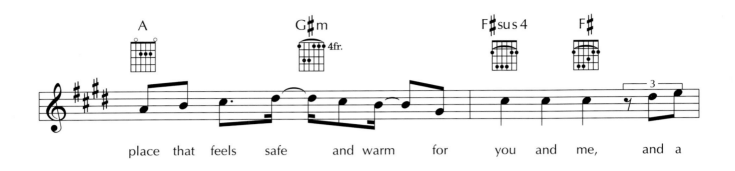

place that feels safe and warm for you and me, and a

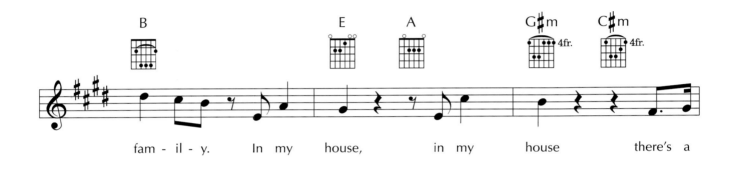

fam - il - y. In my house, in my house there's a

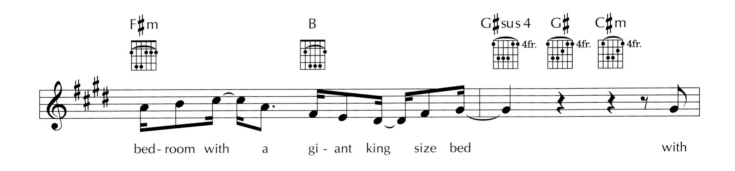

bed - room with a gi - ant king size bed with

two fluf- fy pil - lows and a quilt - ed spread in my

house,   in my   house.   Oh!   In my

house,   in my   house.   Oh!   In my

house,   in my   house.

THE CITY

I love the city,
The sounds and the lights,
The hustle and bustle
From morning til night.
So many people and places to see!
It's where I want to be!
The city life is for me!

Hotels and motels
And skyscrapers tall!
Wonderful restaurants
And big shopping malls!
Museums and theaters,
There's so much to do!
Every day's an adventure that's new!

I love the city,
The sounds and the lights,
The hustle and bustle
From morning til night.
So many people and places to see!
It's where I want to be!
The city life is for me!

Taxis and buses
Move people around.
There's even a subway
That runs underground.
There's a park, and a zoo,
A library, too!
It's a place to make dreams come true!

Oh! I love the city,
The sounds and the lights,
The hustle and bustle
From morning til night.
So many people and places to see!
It's where I want to be!
The city life is for me!

I love the city,
The sounds and the lights.
The city life is for me!

43

THE CITY

I love the _____,
The sounds and the _____,
The hustle and bustle
From _____ til _____.
So many people and _____ to see!
It's where I want to be!
The _____ life is for me!

_____ and motels
And _____ tall!
Wonderful _____
And big _____ _____.
Museums and _____,
There's so much to do!
Every day's an adventure that's new!

I _____ the city,
The _____ and the lights,
The hustle _____ bustle
From morning til night.
So many _____ and places to see!
It's where I want to be!
The city life is for _____!

Taxis and _____
Move people around.
There's even a _____
That runs underground.
There's a _____, and a zoo,
A _____, too!
It's a place to make dreams come true!

RHYME TIME

What's the rhyming word from the song?

1. motel   _____
2. tall   _____
3. new   _____
4. night   _____
5. underground   _____
6. too   _____
7. hustle   _____

I'M ALL MIXED UP!

Unscramble things in the city.

1. ozo   _____
2. ywbsau   _____
3. stolem   _____
4. mumuses   _____
5. trasrentusa   _____
6. shelot   _____
7. susbe   _____
8. karp   _____
9. estethat   _____

I'LL BE HERE FOR YOU

Where in the song can you find these people and things?

1. book   _____
2. animals   _____
3. actress   _____
4. waiter   _____
5. train   _____
6. painting   _____

ABOUT YOU

Tell about a city you love and give the reasons why.

. . . .

. . . .

. . . .

. . . .

. . . .

YOUR SONG

Write a similar song about how you love the country. You can refer to pages 99, 113, 114, and 115 in the *Word by Word Picture Dictionary* for ideas. Sing your song using the sing-along version of "The City" on the *Word by Word Song Album*.

The City

Words and Music by
PETER S. BLISS

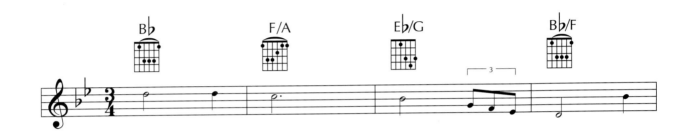

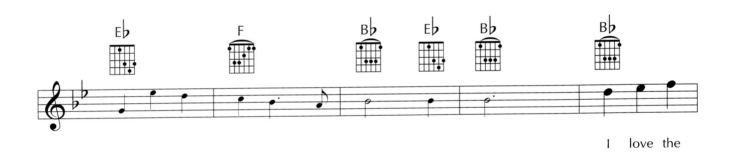

I love the

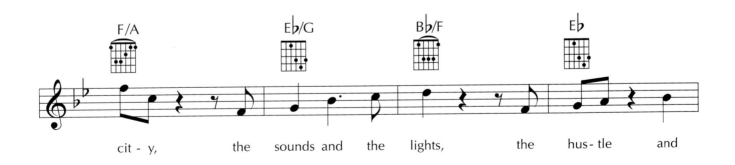

cit - y,   the   sounds and the   lights,   the   hus - tle   and

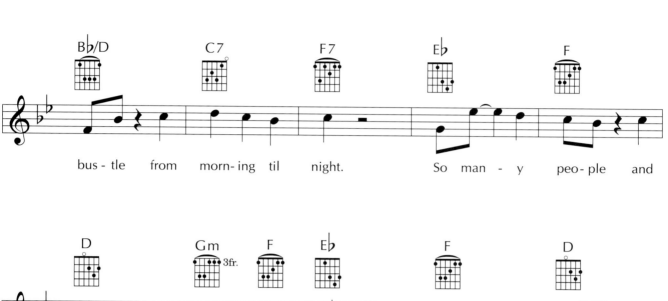

bus - tle from morn- ing til night. So man - y peo - ple and

plac - es to see! It's where I want to be!_____

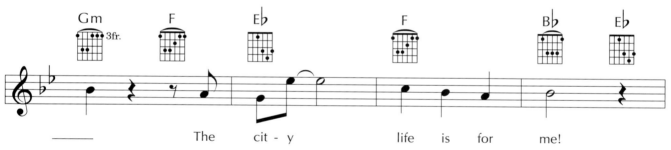

_____ The cit - y life is for me!

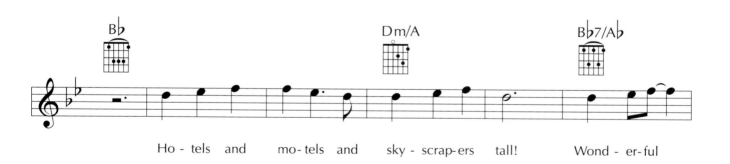

Ho - tels and mo - tels and sky - scrap- ers tall! Wond - er- ful

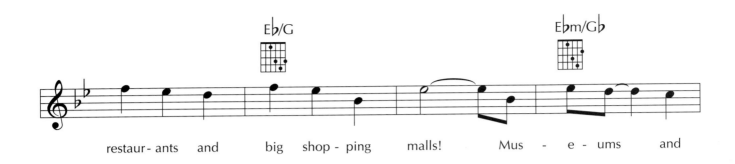

restaur-ants and big shop-ping malls! Mus - e - ums and

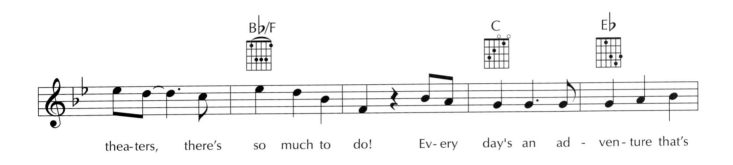

thea-ters, there's so much to do! Ev- ery day's an ad - ven-ture that's

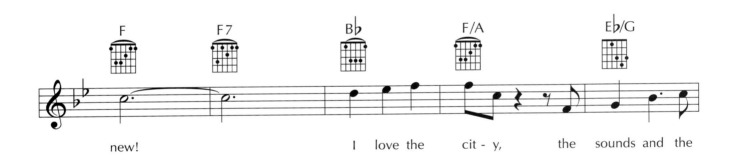

new! I love the cit - y, the sounds and the

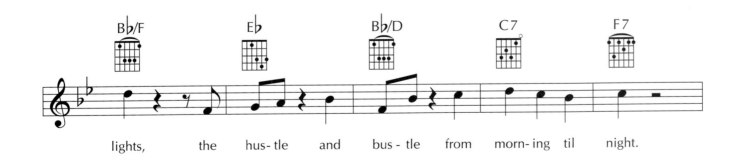

lights, the hus- tle and bus- tle from morn-ing til night.

48

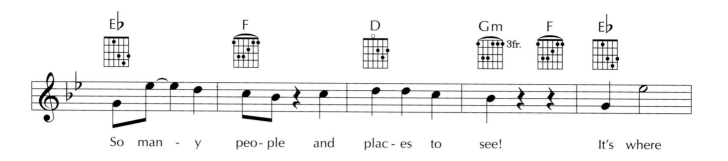

So man - y peo - ple and plac - es to see! It's where

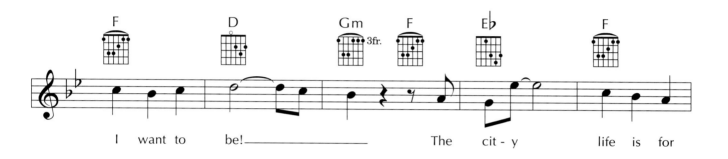

I want to be!_____ The cit - y life is for

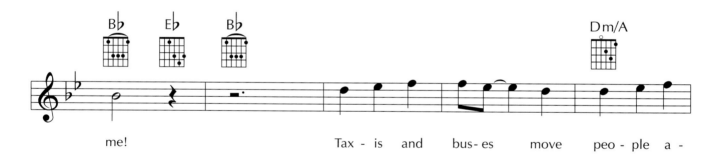

me! Tax - is and bus - es move peo - ple a -

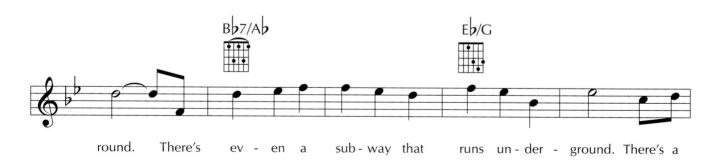

round. There's ev - en a sub - way that runs un - der - ground. There's a

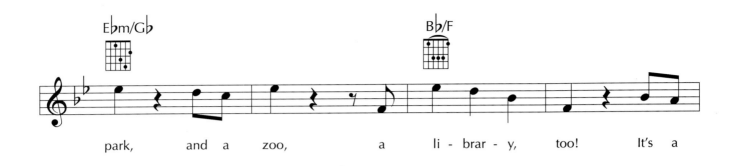

park, and a zoo, a li-brar-y, too! It's a

place to make dreams come true! Oh!_____ I love the

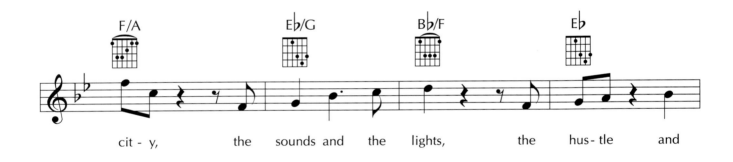

cit - y, the sounds and the lights, the hus-tle and

bus-tle from morn-ing til night. So man - y peo-ple and

places to see! It's where I want to

be! The cit - y life is for

me! I love the cit - y, the sounds and the

lights. The cit - y life is for me!

SUPERMARKET SALLY

(Chorus)
Her name is Supermarket Sally.
She works the checkout line,
Ringing up the groceries
Every day til nine.
She takes my discount coupons.
I save money every time.
Her name is Supermarket Sally.
She's a friend of mine.

I see her every Monday.
That's the day I shop.
My list is always very long.
My cart's filled to the top.

Sally sees me coming.
She stops and waves hello,
Standing at her register.
That's where I always go – o – o!

Chorus

She weighs each fruit and vegetable
On her supermarket scale.
She enters in the price per pound.
She knows just what's on sale.

She knows where every item is
By section and by aisle.
So if you have a question,
Just look for Sally's smile!

Chorus

Her name is Supermarket Sally.
She works the checkout line.
Supermarket Sally!
She's a friend of mine!

SUPERMARKET SALLY

Her _____ is Supermarket Sally.
She works the _____ line,
Ringing up the _____
Every day til nine.
She takes my discount _____.
I save _____ every time.
Her name is Supermarket Sally.
She's a friend of mine.

    I see her every _____.
    That's the day I _____.
    My _____ is always very long.
    My cart's filled to the top.

    Sally sees me coming.
    She stops and waves _____,
    Standing at her _____.
    That's where I always go - o - o!

Her name is _____ Sally.
She works the checkout _____.
_____ up the groceries
Every _____ til nine.
She takes my _____ coupons.
I _____ money every time.
Her name is Supermarket Sally.
She's a friend of mine.

    She weighs each _____ and vegetable
    On her supermarket _____.
    She enters in the price per _____.
    She knows just what's on _____.

    She knows where every item is
    By _____ and by _____.
    So if you have a question,
    Just look for Sally's smile!

RHYME TIME

What's the rhyming word from the song?

1. nine _____
2. top _____
3. sale _____
4. smile _____
5. go _____

WE BELONG TOGETHER

Match the words.

_____ 1. checkout   a. money
_____ 2. price   b. sale
_____ 3. discount   c. per pound
_____ 4. on   d. coupon
_____ 5. wave   e. line
_____ 6. save   f. hello

MISSING YOU

Fill in the missing word from the song.

1. I shop every _____.
2. I fill my _____ with groceries.
3. Sally works every day until _____.
4. I save _____ with my discount coupons.
5. Sally weighs each fruit and _____ on her scale.

ABOUT YOU

Where do you buy groceries? . . . .

Which day do you usually shop? . . . .

Do you make a shopping list? . . . .

Do you use discount coupons? For which products? . . . .

. . . .

What do you do while you're waiting in the checkout line? . . . .

. . . .

Are the people who work there friendly? . . . .

TRY TO REMEMBER

Test your memory. Draw a diagram of the place where you usually buy groceries. Label the aisles and sections and show where items are located. Then visit the store and check your diagram. How well did you remember?

Supermarket Sally

Words and Music by
PETER S. BLISS

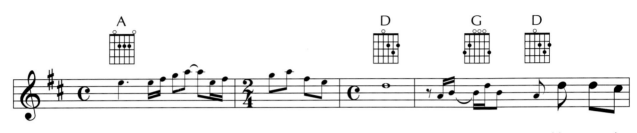

Her name is

Su - per - mar - ket Sal - ly.   She   works   the check-out line,

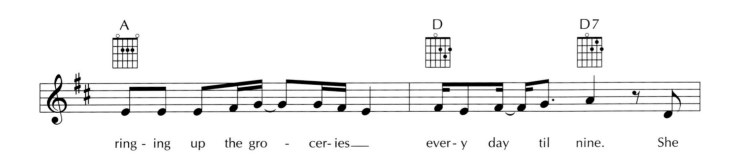

ring - ing   up   the gro - cer - ies____   ev-er - y   day   til   nine.   She

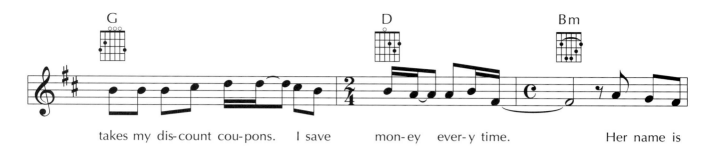

takes my dis-count cou-pons. I save mon-ey ever-y time. Her name is

Su - per-mar - ket Sal - ly. She's a friend of mine.

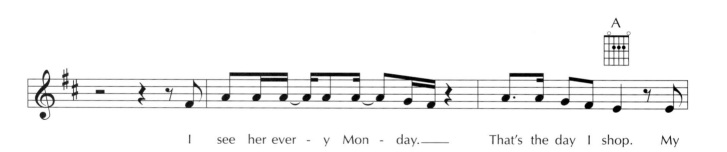

I see her ever - y Mon - day.____ That's the day I shop. My

list is al - ways ver-y long. My cart's filled to the top.

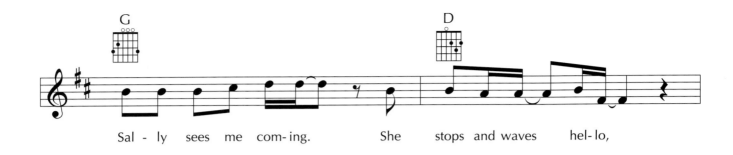

Sal - ly sees me com-ing. She stops and waves hel-lo,

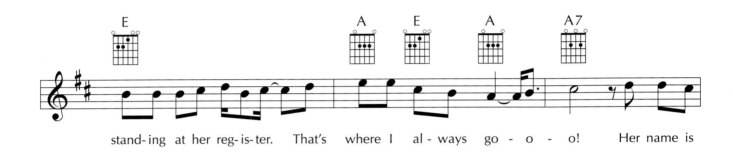

stand-ing at her reg-is-ter. That's where I al-ways go-o-o! Her name is

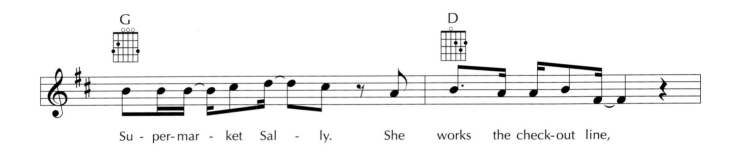

Su - per-mar - ket Sal - ly. She works the check-out line,

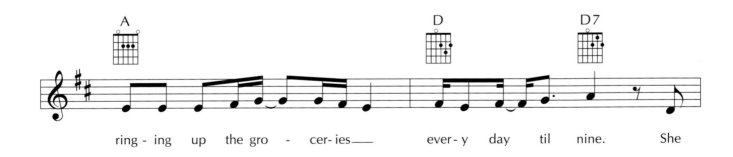

ring-ing up the gro - cer-ies____ ever-y day til nine. She

takes my dis - count cou - pons. I save mon - ey ever - y time.

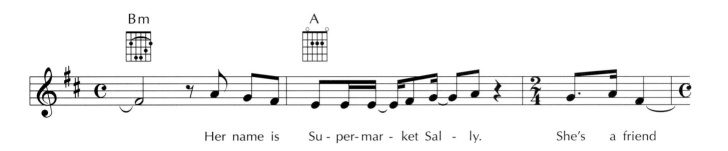

Her name is Su - per - mar - ket Sal - ly. She's a friend

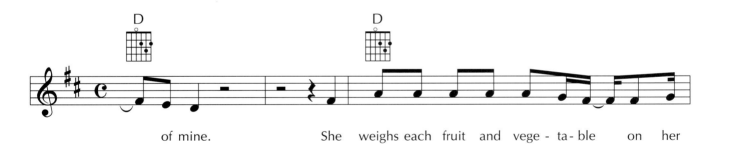

of mine. She weighs each fruit and vege - ta - ble on her

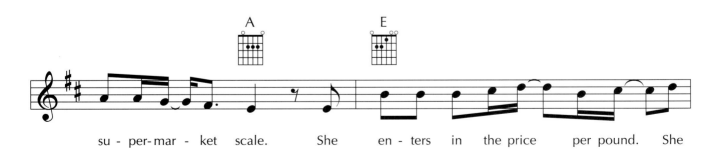

su - per - mar - ket scale. She en - ters in the price per pound. She

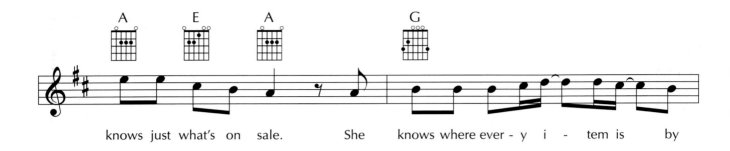

knows just what's on sale. She knows where ever - y i - tem is by

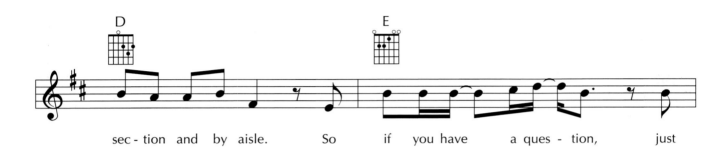

sec - tion and by aisle. So if you have a ques - tion, just

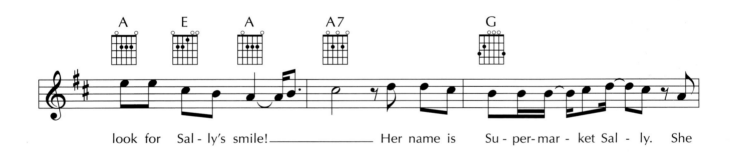

look for Sal - ly's smile!_____ Her name is Su - per - mar - ket Sal - ly. She

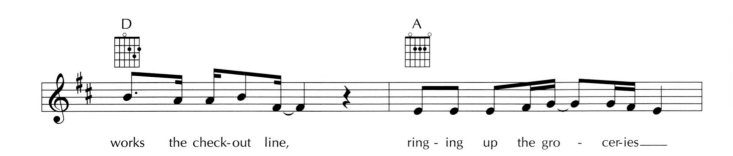

works the check-out line, ring - ing up the gro - cer-ies_____

ever-y day til nine. She takes my dis-count cou-pons. I save mon-ey ever-y time.

Her name is Su - per-mar - ket Sal - ly. She's a friend of

mine. Her name is Su - per-mar - ket Sal - ly. She works the check-out line.

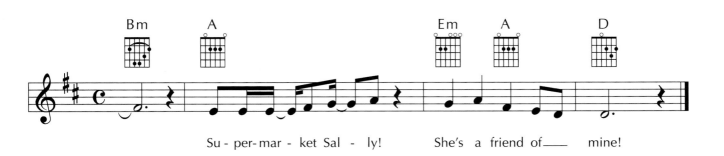

Su - per-mar - ket Sal - ly! She's a friend of___ mine!

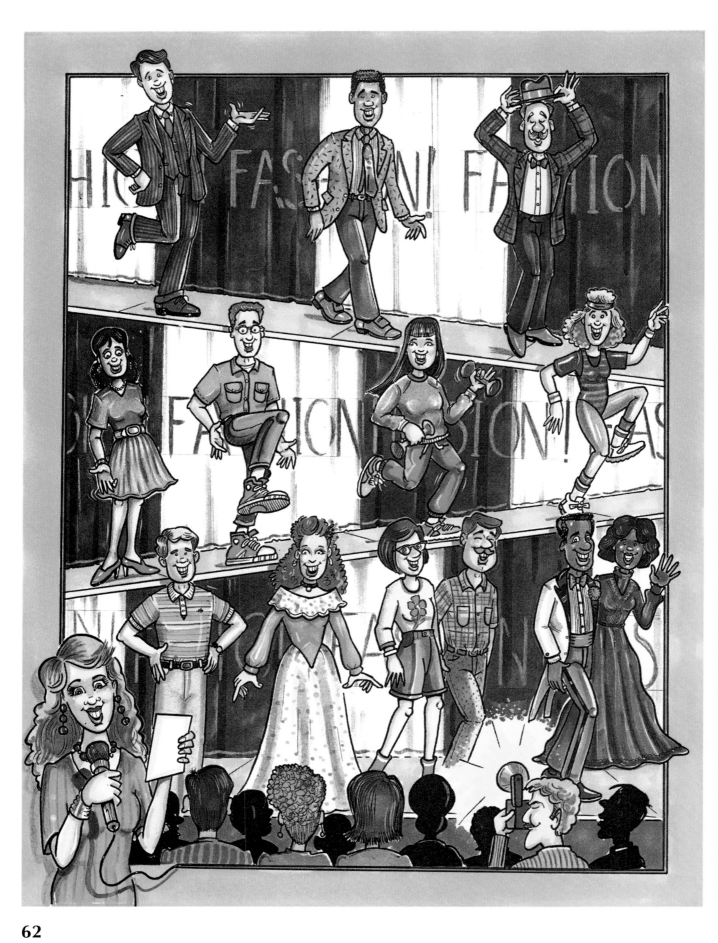

FASHION

(Chorus)
Fashion! Fashion!
It's in the way we look
And the clothes we wear!
Fashion! Oh, fashion!
It's in our style of dress
And the way we comb our hair!
It's fashion! Fashion!

    A three-piece suit!
    A jacket and tie!
    Let's add a hat!
    Let's accessorize!
    Shoes and sneakers!
    There's so much to buy!
    A sweatshirt, a leotard!
    It's time to exercise!

Chorus

    A polo shirt!
    An evening gown!
    Go casual or formal
    For a night on the town!
    Dressing up
    Or dressing down!
    An outfit for the way you feel,
    For walking around!

Chorus (2x)

It's fashion! Fashion!
It's fashion! Fashion!
It's fashion! Fashion!
It's fashion!

FASHION

Fashion! Fashion!
It's in the way we look
And the _____ we wear!
Fashion! Oh, fashion!
It's in our style of dress
And the way we _____ our hair!
It's fashion! Fashion!

    A three-piece _____!
    A _____ and tie!
    Let's add a _____!
    Let's accessorize!
    Shoes and _____!
    There's so much to buy!
    A _____ , a leotard!
    It's time to exercise!

Fashion! Fashion!
It's in the way we _____
And the clothes we _____!
Fashion! Oh, fashion!
It's in our style of _____
And the way we comb our _____!
It's fashion! Fashion!

    A polo _____!
    An evening _____!
    Go casual or formal
    For a night on the _____!
    Dressing up
    Or dressing down!
    An _____ for the way you feel,
    For walking around!

RHYME TIME

What's the rhyming word from the song?

1. wear   _____
2. town   _____
3. buy   _____
4. accessorize   _____

I'M ALL MIXED UP!

Unscramble the clothing items.

1. tha   _____
2. troaled   _____
3. kreenssa   _____
4. takjce   _____
5. hesso   _____
6. trashwestir   _____

ABOUT YOU

Do you like to *dress up* for special occasions? When do you *dress up*? What do you wear?

. . . .

Do you like to wear casual clothes? What do you usually wear?

. . . .

What do you wear when you exercise or do sports?

. . . .

What's *in fashion* now? What styles of dress are popular for men? for women?

. . . .

What *isn't* in fashion now that used to be?

. . . .

Compare fashions in two different cities or two different countries you know.

. . . .

YOUR SONG

Fill in these verses using any clothing items you wish. (You can use pages 57-60 of the *Word by Word Picture Dictionary* for ideas.) Then sing your song using the sing-along version of "Fashion" on the *Word by Word Song Album*.

A/An . . . . !
A/An . . . . and . . . . !
Let's add a/an . . . . !
Let's accessorize!
. . . . and . . . . !
There's so much to buy!
A/An . . . . , a/an . . . . !
It's time to exercise!

A/An . . . . !
A/An . . . . !
Go casual or formal
For a night on the town!
Dressing up
Or dressing down!
An outfit for the way you feel,
For walking around!

Fashion

Words and Music by
PETER S. BLISS

Oh!_____ Oh!_____

Fa - shion!   Fa - shion!   It's   in the way we look and the   clothes we wear!

Fa - shion!   Oh,___ fa - shion!   It's   in our style of dress and the

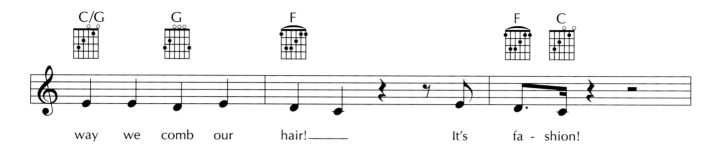

way we comb our hair!_____ It's fa - shion!

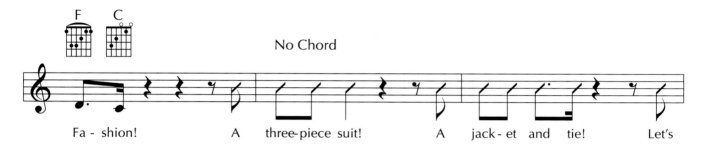

No Chord

Fa - shion! A three-piece suit! A jack - et and tie! Let's

add a hat! Let's ac - ces - sor-ize! Shoes and sneak-ers! There's

so much to buy! A sweat-shirt, a le-o-tard! It's time to ex - er-cise!

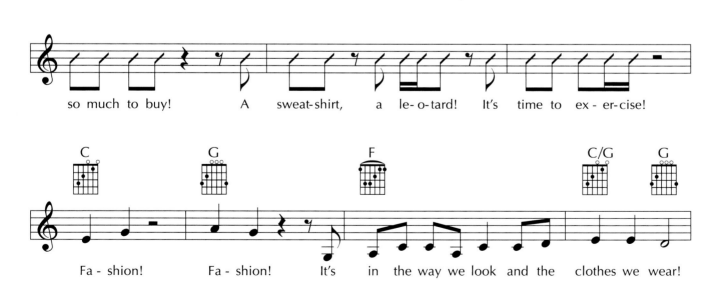

Fa - shion! Fa - shion! It's in the way we look and the clothes we wear!

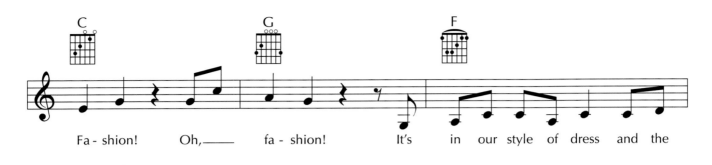

Fa - shion! Oh,_____ fa - shion! It's in our style of dress and the

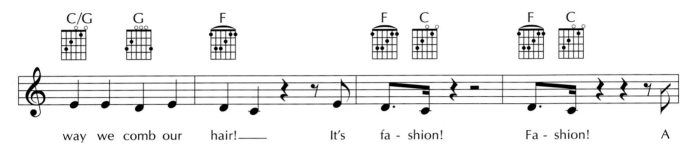

way we comb our hair!_____ It's fa - shion! Fa - shion! A

No Chord

po - lo shirt! An even - ing gown! Go cas - u - al or form - al for a

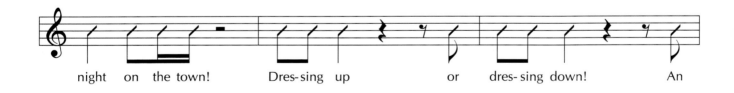

night on the town! Dres - sing up or dres - sing down! An

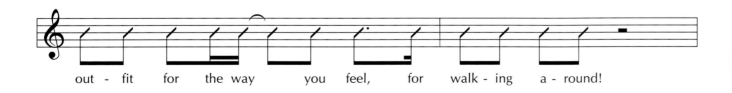

out - fit for the way you feel, for walk - ing a - round!

68

Fa - shion! Fa - shion! It's in the way we look and the

clothes we wear! Fa - shion! Oh,_____ fa - shion! It's

in our style of dress and the way we comb our hair!_____

hair!____ It's fa - shion! Fa - shion! It's fa - shion!

Fa - shion! It's fa - shion! Fa - shion! It's fa - shion!

No Chord

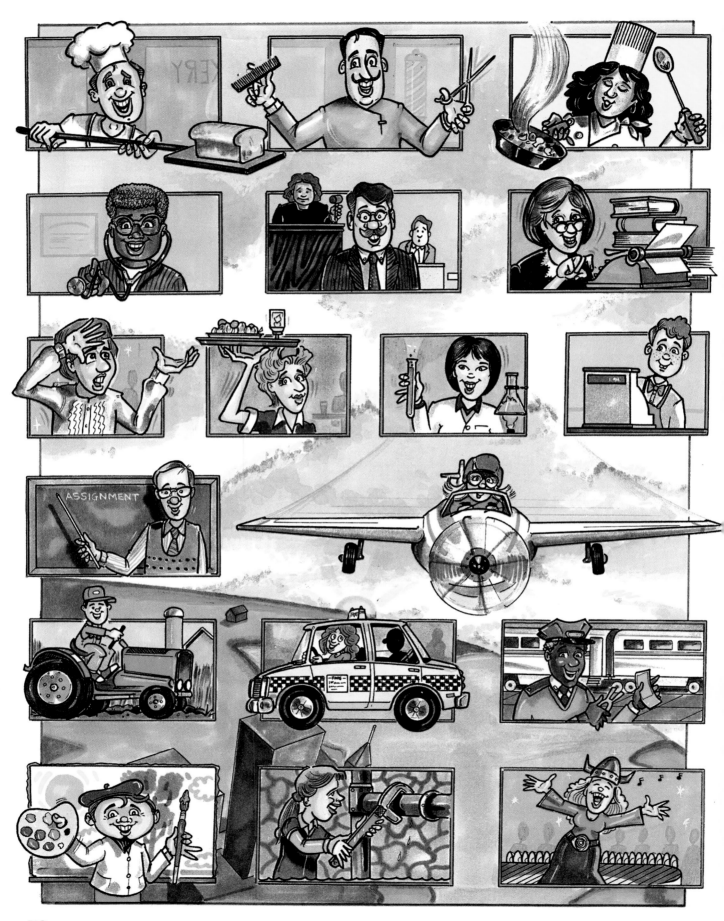

WORKING

(Chorus)
Working! Working!
Everybody's working!
Working! Working!
Working for a living!
Working! Working!
One thing in life is true!
Everybody's got a job to do!
Working!

A baker, a barber,
A chef who likes to cook.
A doctor, a lawyer,
An author writing books.
An actor, a waitress,
A scientist, a clerk.
So many occupations!
So many types of work!

Chorus

A teacher, a pilot,
Flying airplanes.
A farmer, a driver,
A conductor on a train.
An artist, a plumber,
An opera star who sings.
So many occupations!
Everybody does something!

Chorus

WORKING

Working! Working!
Everybody's _____!
Working! Working!
Working for a living!
Working! Working!
One thing in _____ is true!
Everybody's got a _____ to do!
Working!

      A _____, a barber,
      A _____ who likes to cook.
      A doctor, a _____,
      An _____ writing books.
      An actor, a _____,
      A _____, a clerk!
      So many occupations!
      So many types of _____!

Working! Working!
_____'s working!
Working! Working!
Working _____ a living!
Working! Working!
One thing _____ life _____ true!
Everybody's got a job to _____!
Working!

      A _____, a pilot,
      Flying airplanes.
      A farmer, a _____,
      A _____ on a train.
      An artist, a _____,
      An opera star who _____.
      So many _____!
      Everybody does something!

I'M THE ONE

Which people in the song do these things?

1. writes books   _____
2. fixes sinks   _____
3. serves food   _____
4. flies airplanes   _____
5. paints pictures   _____
6. sings   _____
7. cuts hair   _____

I'M ALL MIXED UP!

Unscramble the occupations.

1. aerbk   _____
2. coodrt   _____
3. ourhat   _____
4. stitra   _____
5. fech   _____
6. strewasi   _____
7. trooncccdu   _____

ABOUT YOU

Tell about people you know and their occupations. . . . .
. . . .
. . . .
. . . .

If you could have any job in the world, what would you like to be? Why? . . . .
. . . .
. . . .
. . . .

YOUR SONG

Fill in these verses using any occupations you wish. (You can use pages 80-83 of the *Word by Word Picture Dictionary* for ideas.) Then sing your song using the sing-along version of "Working" on the *Word by Word Song Album*.

A/An . . . ., a/an . . . .,
A chef who likes to cook.
A/An . . . ., a/an . . . .,
An author writing books.
A/An . . . ., a/an . . . .,
A/An . . . ., a clerk.
So many occupations!
So many types of work.

A/An . . . ., a pilot,
Flying airplanes.
A/An . . . ., a/an . . . .,
A conductor on a train.
A/An . . . ., a/an . . . .,
An opera star who sings.
So many occupations!
Everybody does something!

Working

Words and Music by
PETER S. BLISS

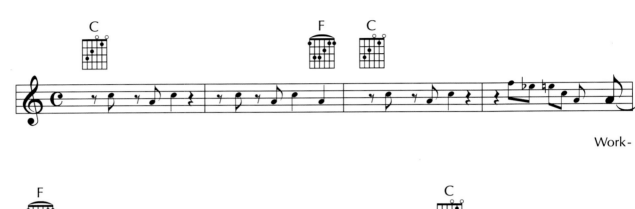

Work-

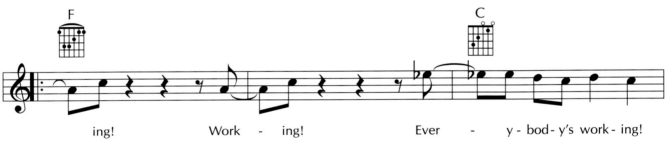

ing! Work - ing! Ever - y - bod - y's work - ing!

Work - ing! Work - ing! Work - ing for a liv - ing!

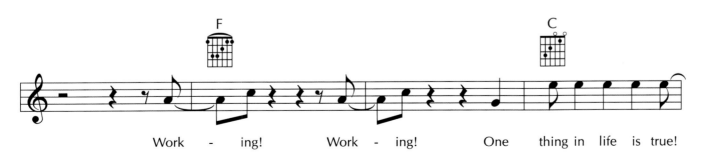

Work - ing! Work - ing! One thing in life is true!

ress,   a   sci - en - tist,____   a   clerk.   So
er,   an   oper - a   star____   who sings.   So

man - y   oc - cu - pa - tions!   So___ man-y types of work!____   Work -
man - y   oc - cu - pa - tions!   Ever-y-bod-y does some-thing!____

ing!   Work   -   ing!   Ever -

y - bod- y's work - ing!   Work   -   ing!   Work -

ing!   Work - ing for a liv - ing!   Work -

ing!   Work - ing!   One   thing   in   life   is   true!

Ever - y - bod - y's   got   a   job——— to do!

Ever-y-bod-y's   got   a   job——— to do!

Ever-y-bod-y's   got   a   job——— to do!

Work - ing!

GOING TO THE BEACH

(Chorus)
We're going to the beach!
We're going to the beach!
We're going to the beach!
Having fun in the sun in the summertime! (2x)

Grab your bathing suit, your surfboard and beach chair!
Let's go where we can smell the ocean air!
Rub on suntan lotion right away.
So we can stay and play at the beach all day!

Chorus (2x)

We'll buy hot dogs at the refreshment stand,
Spread our blankets and picnic on the sand.
When it gets too hot, we'll go for a swim.
We'll have a race to see who'll be the first one in.

We're going to the beach!
We're going to the beach!
We're going to the beach!
Having fun in the sun in the summertime!

We're going to the beach!
We're going to the beach!
We're going to the beach!
Having fun in the sun in the summertime!
Having fun in the sun in the summertime!
Having fun in the sun in the summertime!

GOING TO THE BEACH

We're going to the _____!
We're _____ to the beach!
_____ going to the beach!
Having fun in the _____ in the summertime!

    Grab your _____ _____, your surfboard and beach chair!
    Let's go where we can smell the _____ air!
    Rub on _____ _____ right away.
    So we can stay and _____ at the beach all day!

We're going _____ the beach!
We're going to _____ beach!
We're going to the _____!
Having fun in the sun in the _____!

    We'll buy hot dogs at the _____ _____!
    Spread our _____ and picnic on the _____.
    When it gets too hot, we'll go for a _____.
    We'll have a race to see who'll be the first one in.

_____ going to the beach!
We're going to the _____!
We're _____ to the beach!
Having _____ in the sun in the summertime!

RHYME TIME

What's the rhyming word from the song?

1. air   _____
2. fun   _____
3. away   _____
4. refreshment stand   _____

WE BELONG TOGETHER

Match the words.

____ 1. rub on   a. ocean air
____ 2. have   b. blanket
____ 3. spread   c. suntan lotion
____ 4. smell   d. fun

IS IT TRUE?

Circle True, False, or Maybe.

1. The people in the song live near the beach.   True   False   Maybe
2. They had a picnic at the refreshment stand.   True   False   Maybe
3. They spread sand on their blankets.   True   False   Maybe
4. They ate hot dogs.   True   False   Maybe
5. They brought their surfboards.   True   False   Maybe
6. The singer was the first one in the water.   True   False   Maybe

ABOUT YOU

What do you like to do in warm weather? . . . .
. . . .

Why do you think people should be careful when they *have fun in the sun in the summertime?*
. . . .

Tell about a time you went to the beach: Where did you go? What did you take with you? What did you do there? . . . .
. . . .
. . . .
. . . .

Going to the Beach

Words and Music by
PETER S. BLISS

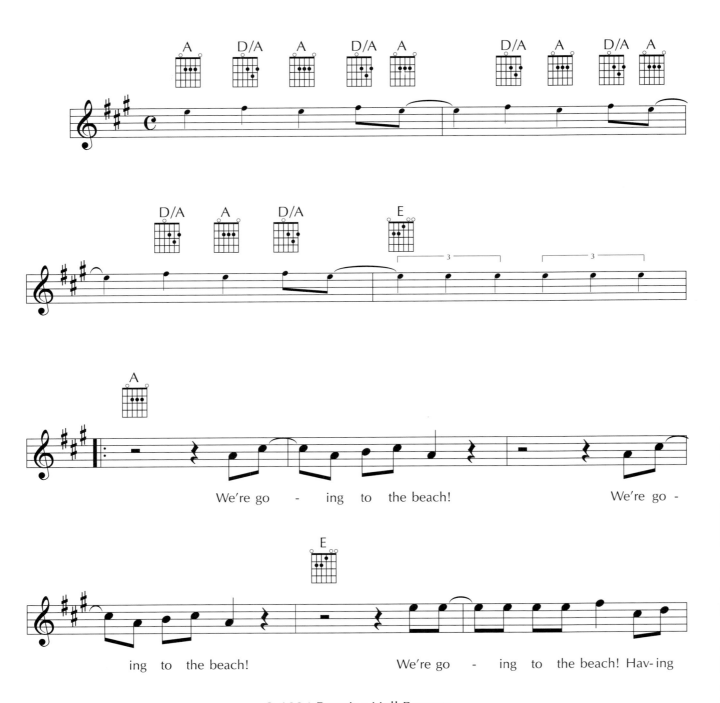

We're go - ing to the beach! We're go -

ing to the beach! We're go - ing to the beach! Hav- ing

fun in the sun in the sum-mer-time!   Grab your bath-ing suit, your

surf-board and beach chair!_____   Let's go where we can smell

the o - cean air!_____   Rub on sun-tan lo -

tion right a-way_____   so we can stay and play

at the beach all day!_____   We're go - ing to the beach!

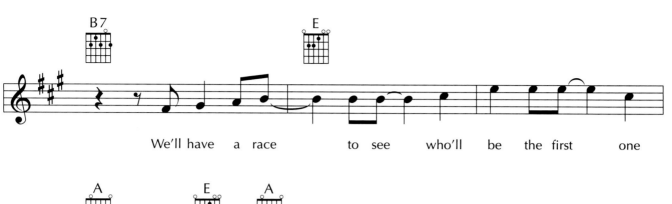

We'll have   a   race   to   see   who'll   be   the   first   one

in._____   We're go - ing to the beach!   We're go-

ing to the beach!   We're go - ing to the beach! Hav- ing   fun in the sun in the

sum- mer - time!   sum- mer - time!   Hav- ing   fun   in   the   sun   in   the

sum- mer - time! Hav- ing fun   in   the sun   in   the   sum- mer   -   time!

POWER UP

(Okay, everybody! Are you ready?
Here we go!
One! Two! Three! Four!)

Let's warm up, bend and stretch!
Let your hands reach for the sky!
Now pick up the pace and run in place!
Feel your heartbeat start to rise!

Working up a sweat, step by step!
Get ready! Get set!

> Everybody, power up! Energize!
> Everybody, power up . . . up . . . up!
> It's time to exercise!
>
> Everybody, power up! Energize!
> Everybody, power up . . . up . . . up!
> It's fun to exercise!
> Everybody, power up!

(Here we go!
One! Two! Three! Four!)

Sit-ups, push-ups, deep knee bends!
Down to the floor, then up again!
Let's bounce the basketball around!
Catch it, kick it, throw it to a friend!

Working up a sweat, step by step!
Get ready! Get set!

> Everybody, power up! Energize!
> Everybody, power up . . . up . . . up!
> It's time to exercise!
>
> Everybody, power up! Energize!
> Everybody, power up . . . up . . . up!
> It's fun to exercise!
>
> Everybody, power up!
> Power up!

POWER UP

Let's warm up, _____ and _____!
Let your hands _____ for the sky!

Now pick up the pace and _____ in place!
Feel your heartbeat start to rise!

Working up a sweat, step by _____!
Get ready! Get set!

    Everybody, power up! Energize!
    Everybody, power up . . . up . . . up!
    It's time to _____!

    Everybody, power up! Energize!
    Everybody, power up . . . up . . . up!
    It's _____ to exercise!
    Everybody, power up!

_____, push-ups, _____ _____ _____!
_____ to the floor, then _____ again!

Let's _____ the basketball around!
_____ it, _____ it, _____ it to a friend!

Working _____ a sweat, step _____ step!
Get ready! Get set!

    Everybody, power up! Energize!
    Everybody, power up . . . up . . . up!
    It's _____ to exercise!

    Everybody, power up! Energize!
    Everybody, power up . . . up . . . up!
    It's fun to _____!

    Everybody, power up!
    Power up!

WE BELONG TOGETHER

Match the words.

____ 1. reach for the   a. pace
____ 2. run in   b. sweat
____ 3. work up a   c. sky
____ 4. pick up the   d. place

WHAT SHOULD I DO?

Number these actions in the correct sequence according to the song.

____ bounce the basketball
____ reach for the sky
____ push-ups
____ run in place
____ bend and stretch
____ deep knee bends
____ sit-ups

IT MAKES NO SENSE TO ME

Check the phrases that *don't* make sense.

____ warm up your heartbeat
____ bounce the basketball
____ throw a friend
____ down to the pace
____ reach for the sky
____ work up a sit-up
____ run in sweat

ABOUT YOU

Do you exercise? How often? Where? What exercises do you do? . . . .
. . . .
. . . .
. . . .
. . . .

Why do you think it's important to *work up a sweat?* . . . .
. . . .
. . . .
. . . .
. . . .

Power Up

Words and Music by
PETER S. BLISS

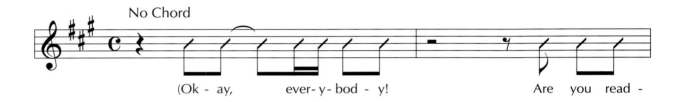

(Ok - ay, ever-y-bod-y! Are you read-

y? Here we go! One! Two! Three! Four!)

Let's warm up, bend and stretch! Let your hands___ reach

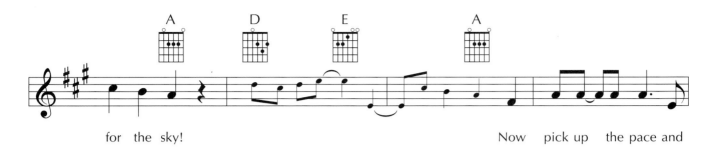

for the sky!   Now   pick up   the pace and

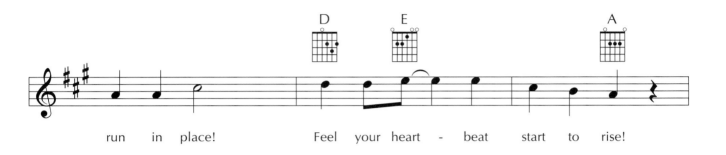

run   in place!   Feel   your   heart - beat   start   to   rise!

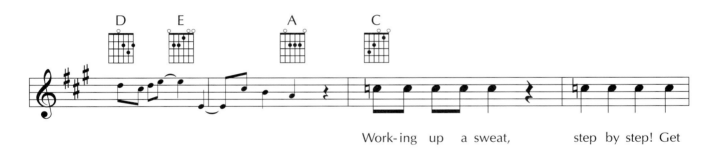

Work-ing   up   a sweat,   step   by step! Get

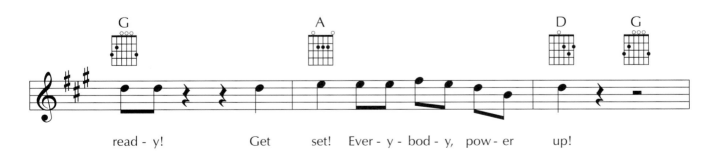

read - y!   Get   set! Ever - y - bod - y, pow - er   up!

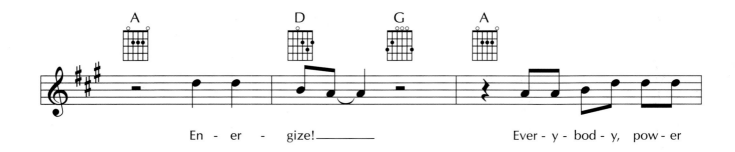

En - er - gize!_____ Ever - y - bod - y, pow - er

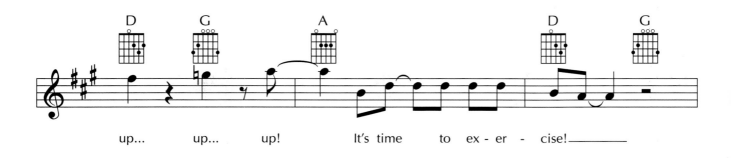

up... up... up! It's time to ex - er - cise!_____

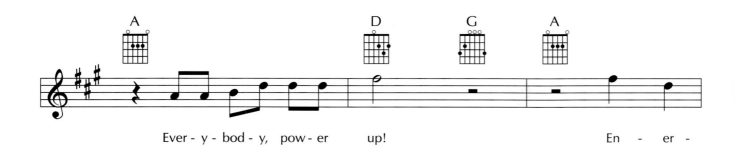

Ever - y - bod - y, pow - er up! En - er -

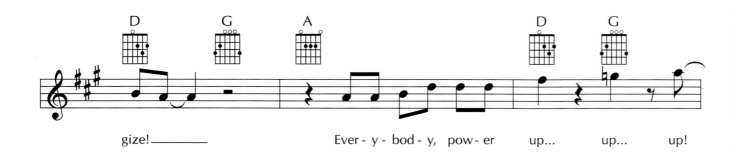

gize!_____ Ever - y - bod - y, pow - er up... up... up!

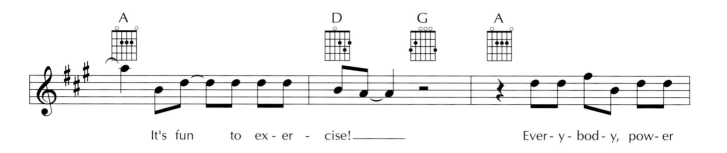

It's fun to ex - er - cise!_____ Ever- y - bod- y, pow- er

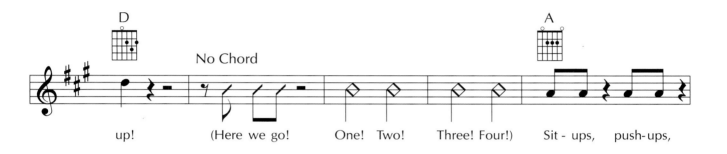

up! (Here we go! One! Two! Three! Four!) Sit - ups, push-ups,

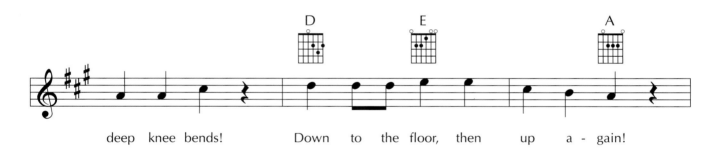

deep knee bends! Down to the floor, then up a - gain!

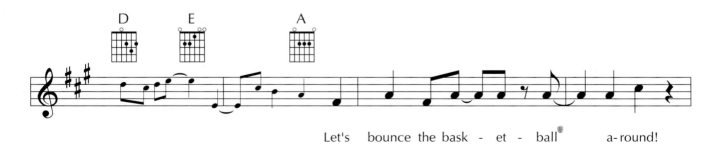

Let's bounce the bask - et - ball a-round!

Catch it, kick it, throw it to a friend!

Work-ing up a sweat, step by step! Get

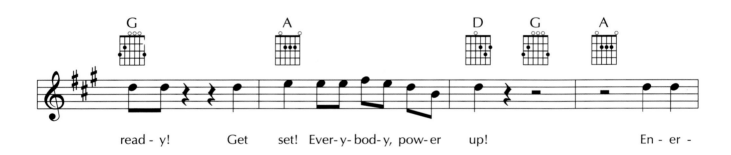

read-y! Get set! Ev-er-y-bod-y, pow-er up! En-er-

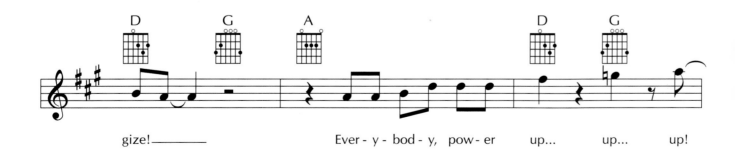

gize!_____ Ev-er-y-bod-y, pow-er up... up... up!

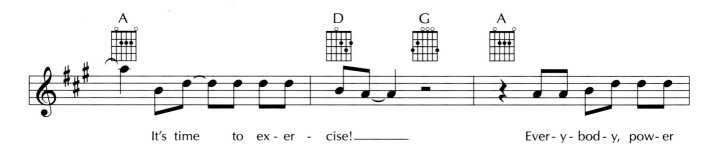

It's time to ex-er - cise!———— Ever-y-bod-y, pow-er

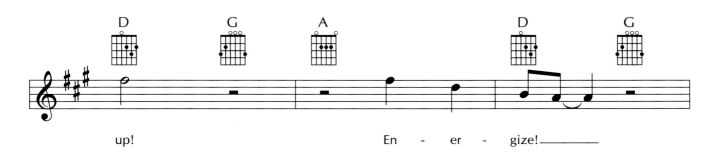

up! En - er - gize!————

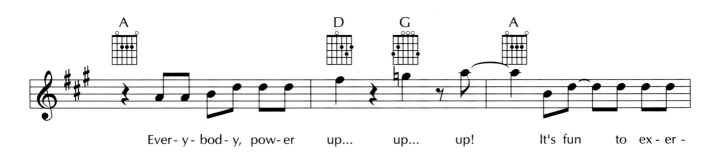

Ever-y-bod-y, pow-er up... up... up! It's fun to ex-er-

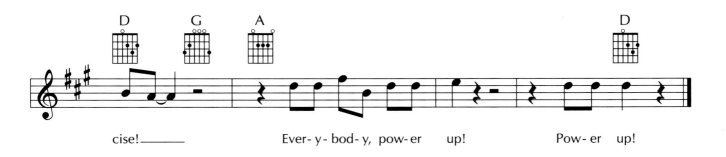

cise!——— Ever-y-bod-y, pow-er up! Pow-er up!

WORD BY WORD
(The Language Learner's Theme)

(Chorus)
Word by word! Word by word!
We bring the world a little closer together.
Word by word! Word by word!
We discover we're all sisters and brothers,
Learning about each other . . . word by word!

Saying "hello" with a smile
Is a language everyone can understand.
Word by word, we're creating
A new way for everyone to all join hands.

Chorus

Look how the earth is getting smaller!
Now there aren't any far-off distant lands.
We've become a world of neighbors,
Sharing hopes and dreams all people understand.

Chorus

So many faces from places far away!
Word by word, we make new friends . . . day by day!

Chorus

We discover we're all sisters and brothers,
Learning about each other . . . word by word!

Word by Word

Words and Music by
PETER S. BLISS

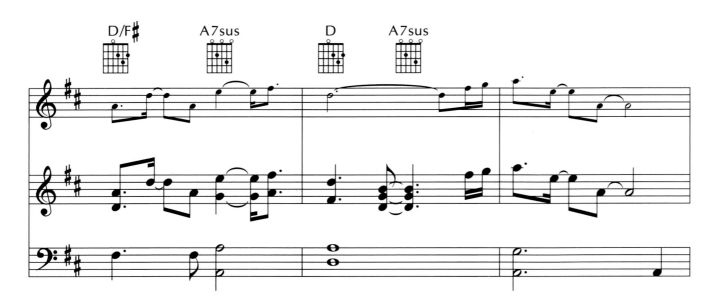

ANSWER KEY

Page 5

WHAT CAN I SAY?
1. Hello.
2. How do you do?
3. I'd like to introduce myself to you.

I'M ALL MIXED UP!
1. father
2. aunt
3. niece
4. uncle
5. mother
6. sister
7. nephew
8. brother

Page 15

IS IT TRUE?
1. False
2. True
3. False
4. True
5. False

Page 25

IS IT TRUE?
1. False
2. True
3. False
4. True
5. True

RHYME TIME
1. day
2. radio
3. watch TV
4. store

WE BELONG TOGETHER
1. f
2. d
3. b
4. e
5. a
6. c

Page 35

WHERE CAN I FIND YOU?
1. bedroom
2. kitchen
3. bathroom
4. living room
5. kitchen, dining room
6. kitchen
7. bedroom
8. living room

IT MAKES NO SENSE TO ME
✔ 1.
___ 2.
___ 3.
✔ 4.
___ 5.
✔ 6.

Page 45

RHYME TIME!
1. hotel
2. mall
3. do
4. light
5. around
6. zoo, true
7. bustle

I'M ALL MIXED UP!
1. zoo
2. subway
3. motels
4. museums
5. restaurants
6. hotels
7. buses
8. park
9. theaters

I'LL BE HERE FOR YOU
1. library
2. zoo
3. theater
4. restaurant
5. subway
6. museum

Page 55

RHYME TIME
1. mine
2. shop
3. scale
4. aisle
5. hello

WE BELONG TOGETHER
1. e
2. c
3. d
4. b
5. f
6. a

MISSING YOU
1. Monday
2. cart
3. nine
4. money
5. vegetable

Page 65

RHYME TIME
1. hair
2. gown
3. tie
4. exercise

I'M ALL MIXED UP!
1. hat
2. leotard
3. sneakers
4. jacket
5. shoes
6. sweatshirt

106

Page 73

I'M THE ONE

1. author	5. artist
2. plumber	6. opera star
3. waitress	7. barber
4. pilot	

I'M ALL MIXED UP!

1. baker	5. chef
2. doctor	6. waitress
3. author	7. conductor
4. artist	

Page 81

RHYME TIME

| 1. chair | 3. day |
| 2. sun | 4. sand |

WE BELONG TOGETHER

| 1. c | 3. b |
| 2. d | 4. a |

IS IT TRUE?

1. Maybe	4. True
2. False	5. True
3. False	6. Maybe

Page 89

WE BELONG TOGETHER

| 1. c | 3. b |
| 2. d | 4. a |

WHAT SHOULD I DO?

7
2
4
3
1
6
5

IT MAKES NO SENSE TO ME

✔

✔
✔

✔
✔

Songbook/Picture Dictionary Correlation

Song	Topic	Word by Word Songbook Pages	Word by Word Picture Dictionary Pages	Word by Word Basic Pages
What's Your Name?	Personal Information and Family Members	2–11	1–3	2–7
Great Big World	Countries, Nationalities, and Languages	12–21	4–8	168–171
Another Day	Everyday Activities	22–31	9–10	8–11
In My House	Rooms in the Home	32–41	14–22	20–35
The City	Places Around Town	42–51	34–39	56–67
Supermarket Sally	Food Shopping	52–61	44–51	76–91
Fashion	Clothing	62–69	57–61	100–109
Working	Occupations and Work Activities	70–77	80–85	138–149
Going to the Beach	Recreation	78–85	101	
Power Up	Sport and Exercise Actions	86–95	108	
Word by Word	"The Language Learner's Theme"	96–105		